T0337272

Bound to Please

Sarah K is the author of *Sunday Times* bestsellers *The Secret Life of a Submissive* and *Bonds of Love*.

Bound to Please

More secrets of a submissive

Sarah K

Harper
True*Desire*

HarperTrueDesire
An imprint of HarperCollins*Publishers*
1 London Bridge Street,
London SE1 9GF

www.harpertrue.com
www.harpercollins.co.uk

First published by HarperTrueDesire 2014

A catalogue record of this book is
available from the British Library

PB ISBN: 978-0-00-810567-9
EB ISBN: 978-0-00-758543-4

Chapter One

I have always thought there is something incredibly sexy about a man in a dinner jacket and bow tie, cummerbund, the whole evening suit thing; and the way Adam's DJ fitted him – making the most of those broad shoulders, narrow waist and long legs – proved my point. His tie was undone now and draped around his muscular neck, his shirt undone a button or two to reveal a light tan and just the hint of a hairy chest. He had the nicest, bluest eyes I've ever seen, their colour accentuated by the black velvet mask he was wearing to cover the top half of his face. Not quite knowing who he was and what he looked like added another layer of excitement.

'Is that okay? Not too tight?' he asked as he tied my wrists together with a wide, red, soft silk ribbon.

'Yes, thank you, Sir,' I answered politely.

He did a double take and then laughed. 'Impressive,' he said. 'Are you always this well behaved?'

I raised an eyebrow. 'What do you think?'

Adam, deadpan, said, 'Maddie told me you and I would get on. I like a subbie with a bit of fight. You're happy? And you're okay with the safe word?'

I nodded. 'Yes,' I said, well aware that Doms don't take a nod for an answer.

'Good,' he said. 'You know you're safe here with me, don't you? If you call a halt, then that's it. We stop.'

'Yes, Sir,' I said.

As our gaze met I could see the little flame of desire in Adam's eyes and knew that it was echoed in mine. I could already feel myself responding to his delight at having a willing woman all tied up and ready for his pleasure – not to mention her own.

In the centre of the room, suspended from the ceiling, was a length of stainless-steel chain with a hook on it that could be adjusted up or down depending on the height of the person being restrained. Adam led me over to it, took the chain and clipped the hook through the silk between my wrists and adjusted it so that my hands were above my head – not quite at full stretch but close to it.

'Comfortable?' Adam asked as I adjusted my position.

'Yes, Sir,' I said.

'Good,' he said. 'You look fabulous.' He paused, holding my gaze so that there could be no misunderstanding. 'And you're happy?'

I nodded. The truth was I wouldn't be here if I wasn't happy, and while it might not suit everyone, this is my idea of having a good time. There was no obligation for me to play, and none at all for me to submit to Adam – it was my choice entirely and I was very happy with this particular evening's decision.

Adam walked around me slowly, taking his time, watching me, taking in every detail, as if I was an unexpected and very special present and he was considering where to begin the unwrapping process. Stepping closer, Adam pressed his lips into the angle of my neck and kissed me. The first touch ricocheted through my body, creating a wave of intense pleasure and expectation. And then he began nipping, licking and kissing, biting – tiny, searing red-hot bites – the brush of his mask providing an odd contrast to the sensation of his lips and tongue and teeth working down over my skin. I groaned and stretched up towards him, keen to enjoy each caress.

Stopping for a moment, Adam leaned in closer. 'Here, let me take your earrings off,' he said, gently tipping my head to one side. 'I'm worried I might catch them.'

I smiled up at him. It was an intimate, caring thing to do, at odds with what most people would associate with Doms and subs and BDSM, but typical of my experience.

'That's better. I'll look after them for you, keep them safe,' he said, slipping them into his jacket pocket. 'Now, where were we?'

Guessing that he was talking to himself, I didn't reply. His lips returned to my neck, working busily up over my throat, nibbling at my ears, breathing me in, and then they worked lower, across my shoulders, down over my collarbones, each kiss, each breath building my expectation and excitement. Finally, Adam reached down and undid the zipper that fastened the corset I was wearing and freed my breasts. His mouth was there an instant behind his fingers.

I gasped as he drew a hard dark nipple deep into his mouth, while his fingers worked at my other breast, nipping and twisting, sharp tiny pains, cupping the soft flesh in the palm of his hand, making me shiver and gasp at the heady mix of pleasure and pain. I could hear and feel his soft murmurs of delight reverberate through my skin as he bit down harder. Gasping at the intensity of the sensations, I pressed my body into his.

It had been a while since I'd played with anyone. Max, my previous partner, had been an accomplished lover and Dom, introducing me to the mysteries and the magic of BDSM. Since we'd split up I had missed the intimacy of our relationship, both mental and physical. The relationship between Master and submissive is an intense, intoxicating mix of trust and emotion, exposing the deepest and most intimate desires of the people involved. Playing with Adam felt like rain after a long drought. I could feel my whole body responding hungrily to each caress, each touch igniting tiny glowing sparks of arousal.

Adam closed his teeth, biting down onto my nipple, making me whimper and gasp, making me writhe with pleasure. He slid a hand between my legs, moving it rhythmically, stroking and pressing up into the crease of my sex under my panties, teasing, changing the pressure and the angle to breathtaking effect, his thumb brushing across my clitoris, his fingers separated from my moist, aching flesh by a triangle of soft leather. I moaned and moved with him, chasing his caress.

His lips moved higher, nibbling my shoulders, gently biting my neck. I closed my eyes, relishing every touch.

Adam pulled away and traced the outline of my mask with his fingertips. 'You are beautiful,' he murmured.

'Thank you,' I whispered. 'You too,' I added with a smile.

There is something empowering and exciting about living out your fantasies. There, right then, I truly felt beautiful, glamorous and mysterious, behind the black silk cat mask. I'd taken the time to put my hair up into a French knot and was wearing a fabulous boned black leather corset, which accentuated my curves, along with a matching G-string, fishnet stockings and high heels. This was all worn with a layered, black-net petticoat studded with tiny diamanté chips that echoed the ornate dangly earrings now safely tucked away in Adam's jacket pocket. Oh, and I was wearing red lipstick – lots of fabulous red lipstick – because in my everyday life, unmasked, away from BDSM and at my desk, I would never think to wear it. Tonight, though, with the corset and the mask, it looked and felt perfect. Tonight, I had the feeling that I could be anyone and anything I wanted, and there is a joy and an added frisson in anonymity and reinvention.

This was one of my first big nights for some time. Max was a hard act to follow, and I couldn't imagine going back to the world of vanilla relationships and vanilla sex. It isn't that vanilla can't be good; it's just that once you've tasted the pleasures of BDSM it's hard to go back, and impossible to *unknow* what you've learnt about yourself and the people you have shared the journey with. For me, guided by Max, my sortie into BDSM had taken me to a place where I had been able to explore my own needs and desires in a safe and exhilarating way, and the experience had an intensity and intimacy that I had never had in a vanilla relationship.

So, as I said, Max was a hard act to follow. I had been looking for a new Master for a while – it wasn't something I planned to rush – when I got a phone call from Maddie, a Dominatrix I had met a couple of times while I was seeing Max. She and her husband liked to get together with other couples for parties and dinners with a strong BDSM element. Hers was a place where birds of the BDSM feather could flock together and play, drink, relax and have fun.

'So how are things?' she said after saying hello.

'Fine –' I said, not knowing quite how much she knew about Max and me.

'Great. I'm just ringing to ask if you and Max would like to come to a party –'

I was about to launch into the *we're-not-together-any-more* speech when she said, 'It's a special party for a special birthday. Although I'm not telling anyone which one. I'd love it if you could make it. I rang Max but I think he must have changed his number.'

'He has,' I said.

'Have you got it?' she asked. 'I'll update my phone book.'

'I'm afraid not. We split up a little while back.' I didn't explain how hard it had been or how messy, but I did say that he had decided to go back to his previous partner.

Maddie was quiet for a moment or two and then she said, 'I'm so sorry. I thought you two were fab together. So how are you doing?'

Where to begin? 'Starting over. Looking for someone new,' I said.

'So have you found anyone else?'

'No. I've met a few guys but –' I left the phrase hanging.

'Well, there you are then,' said Maddie. 'Why don't you come to the party anyway? It would be great to see you. I'm just thinking who I can invite that might interest you,' she added mischievously.

'That's really kind but I'm not really sure about coming on my own.'

'Oh come on, you'll be fine,' said Maddie. 'I'll look after you, I promise – and we've got some lovely people coming. I think you'll probably know quite a few of them already. There's going to be good food, champagne, dancing. And there's plenty of room for you to stay over if you wanted to have a drink.' She paused. When I didn't reply she added, 'You really should come, Sarah. Where better to find a new Dom than at a BDSM party? Come on, say you'll come. There'll be lots of people who've come to play and you don't have to join in if you'd prefer to watch. You know that. And we've got some other singles coming. It'll be a chance to dress up and have some fun.'

I smiled; Maddie was really selling it.

'Come on,' she pressed. 'It'll be fun.'

Which was why I now found myself tied up in one of Maddie's bedrooms, with a man I barely knew, but whom Maddie assured me was a complete pussycat.

A pussycat with a real gleam in his eye and a tongue that was making every inch of me tingle.

The bedroom Adam and I were in was dominated by a large mirrored wardrobe that ran along one wall and gave a perfect view of what was going on between the two of us. I found myself watching Adam's attentions as he moved across my body, while feeling his tongue and lips on my throat, and the nip of his teeth. It is odd to see what is going on as well as to feel it, and it added another layer of excitement and expectation, as I became both an observer and a participant. It was compelling viewing.

Adam cupped my breast, nipping the dark peak between his thumb and forefinger, rolling it, tugging at it, while the woman in the mirror, her hands fastened above her head, gasped at the sensation. She looked mysterious and exotic in her mask, her skin slightly flushed, eyes bright with desire, as she moved under Adam's knowing touch.

I smiled at her and she smiled back.

Adam caught my gaze and nodded. 'Admiring yourself?' he said, and then before I could reply, he continued, 'Why don't I give you something worth watching?'

He picked up a riding crop from among a selection of toys on a side table and flexed it, bending it into an arc before taking a couple of practice swings to gauge the heft. He slipped off his jacket, took out his cufflinks and rolled up his sleeves and tried again.

Sarah K

The shaft cut through the air with a distinctive and familiar sound that made me flinch.

Adam smiled at my reaction and then teased the leather tongue at the end of the crop across my hardened nipples before gently flicking them, making them tingle and throb. Circling me, he stroked down over my ribs with the leather shaft, then my stomach, my waist, up across my shoulders, my back, my bottom, my thighs. With every caress I was anticipating the crack and the sting, not the gentle kiss of its tongue. Its touch, his cool, considered attentions and the waiting made me shiver, made me ache, made me hungry for more, and then finally I closed my eyes, shutting out my reflection, full of expectation for what must surely follow.

Was that the moment Adam had been waiting for, the moment I closed out the world and concentrated on him alone and the crop and what they could give? The moment I surrendered I felt the crop moving away and an instant later the hot wild sting as it found its mark across my back. I gasped, jerking against my restraints, as every nerve ending in my body lit up. The blow wasn't hard, but it was enough to make me focus on what was happening, turning my eye inward.

Before I could gather my thoughts the crop hit home again. I cried out as much from surprise as any pain, bucking and gasping for air. The stroke was still not particularly hard but it hurt nonetheless; the sensation left me breathless. I had forgotten what being cropped felt like, how sharp and how cruel the feeling, the sensations rippling out like lava from the point of contact. Despite being a subbie I'm not naturally drawn to pain; it is only here in the BDSM arena where I understand that it is a means to an end that is why I seek it out. I am torn between loving and loathing how it feels. The truth is that pain takes me to a place I can't reach any other way, but even so I find it hard to ride the waves that lead me there.

'Can you count?' Adam whispered in my ear as he leant in so close that I could feel his breath on my skin.

'Two,' I whispered thickly, my voice almost lost in among the clamour of sensations.

'Very good,' he purred, and then I heard the crop cut through the air again and braced myself, knowing what was coming next. The blow was fractionally harder this time, the sensation more acute; I gasped and threw back my head, pulling hard on the restraints.

'Too much?' he asked.

'No,' I whispered. 'No.'

'That's good,' he said, and I could hear the delight in his voice, the pleasure and the arousal.

'Three,' I said.

I wondered how many strokes Adam had planned. It's not that I was afraid of not being able to cope – I knew that if it became too much then I could call a halt – it's just that, as I said, it had been a while and my body had forgotten how intense the crop felt. I knew full well that if Adam could read me, if there was a gentle build-up, the lashes growing in intensity, stroke on stroke, then my body would flood with endorphins so heady and so intoxicating that they are almost addictive. I didn't want it to be too intense too soon, so that I would feel the need to stop.

The crop hit home again. I gasped and flexed instinctively against the chain.

'Four,' I hissed on an outward breath. I could feel my body beginning to embrace the sensation – chasing it, losing myself in it. There is no pretence with pain, no way of hiding from its effects. With my eyes closed tight, each stroke is like an arc of white-hot sparks exploding through my mind, clear as a shooting star.

I realised how much I had missed this, how much I'd missed Max, how much I had missed the ritual and games of BDSM, as well as the intense and heady sensations that the lifestyle brings, and that feeling of being part of something bigger, something special, something all-engulfing.

The lightning struck again and I cried out.

'Five.' I was trembling now. My voice was thick with emotion, not from pain but from a deep, deep longing.

'Six.' The voice no longer sounded like mine.

And then there was silence. My whole body tingled and throbbed. I opened my eyes to see that Adam was still standing behind me with the crop in his hand. He was watching me in the mirror. His eyes were bright with desire and pure animal excitement. His identity might be a mystery but his arousal was anything but hidden; he practically glowed with it. He began to kiss my back, his lips and tongue tracing what I guessed had to be the welts – the long raised pink stripes – made by the crop. His kisses were tender, his touch electrifying. I could feel my whole body responding to his caress, a low dull hunger already building deep inside.

'Do you want more?' Adam asked. He paused and stood up, his gaze meeting mine as his hands circled me to cup and tease my breasts. Caught up in the moment, I nodded.

He smiled wolfishly. 'You have to ask.'

I stared at him.

He laughed. 'Come on, you know the rules.'

'Please,' I said, struggling to find my voice.

'Please what, Sarah?'

'Please may I have some more, Sir?'

'Good girl. How many more strokes do you want?'

Oh sweet torture to be asked just how much pain you would like. 'Four,' I said. It would take it up to ten; ten would be enough, I thought.

He didn't ask me again. The next sound I heard was the shaft of the crop cutting through the still air.

The stroke was harder still and lower, across the swell of my bottom. I bucked and shrieked, stamping my feet at how much it stung.

'Seven, seven,' I gabbled.

I heard him chuckle as he drew the crop back again. I closed my eyes, trying to remind myself that I had asked for this. I heard him change position for the next stroke. Eight caught me lower across the back of the thighs and made me gasp it stung so very much.

Nine was higher, across my back, and ten was full-on, a great cracking stroke across the curve of my backside, and I counted them all, lost now in an abstracted sea of sensations.

But finally Adam was done, and, dropping the crop, he gently unfastened my wrists and guided me over to the bed, his hands exploring my body as he pressed me back among the crush of cushions and pillows. The pain had stilled my racing mind, making me calm all the way through to my core. He slid his fingers under the sides of my G-string, and I lifted my hips to help him take it off. As he slipped it off he parted my legs, gently pushing his hand up between my thighs, opening me up, exposing me to his desire.

And all the while Adam was kissing my breasts, sucking my nipples, while his fingers were eager to explore the moist folds of my sex. I gasped as he slipped a finger inside me, his thumb brushing my clitoris. I lifted my pelvis eagerly. He made a soft throaty noise of appreciation before his kisses moved lower and lower, his tongue tracing a path down between my breasts, over my ribs, kissing and licking my navel and the sensitive skin in the bowl of my belly beneath my hip bones and the inside of my thighs. His kisses were feather-light, delicate, exciting, like a scattering of petals across my body. He worked lower still, kissing the creamy-white flesh above my stocking tops before unfastening and peeling each one off, his fingers and tongue working their way down to my knees, my ankles. Then he was slipping off my shoes and licking and sucking my toes.

The sensation was mind-blowing and made me tremble with delight. Moving back up, he kissed each of the little cascade of stars I have tattooed on my ankle and then very slowly worked his way back up until his lips and tongue finally found the soft, eager swell of my sex.

By the time his tongue found my clitoris my whole body was baying for release, but it was worth the wait. Adam was beyond good. I moaned with sheer pleasure as his knowing tongue set to work, bringing me closer and closer to the edge, working my clitoris with tiny fluttering tip-of-the-tongue caresses, fast, now slow, sucking, circling, and then long lapping strokes with his whole tongue. The growing sensations were driving me crazy.

I could feel my body responding, feel the desire and the excitement building and building as his tongue lapped on and on, ceaselessly teasing at my clitoris, while his fingers worked rhythmically in and out, pressing and stroking my G-spot, the edge of his mask brushing my thighs as I began to move with him, matching his fingers and tongue stroke for stroke.

He was playing me like a finely tuned instrument and I was totally caught up in the moment. Drunk with excitement, I was chasing release now, riding a great tidal surge of arousal, desperate to come, aching to tumble over the edge into oblivion, lifting my hips, wanton and hungry for more.

As the first ripples rolled through me I moaned with pure ecstasy, my fingers locked into his hair, holding onto him, begging him not to stop, imploring him to carry on, more, more – and that was exactly what he gave me until, finally, totally sated, I fell back onto the bed, breathing hard.

Pulling away, Adam sat back on his heels and grinned down at me.

'For a submissive you're very demanding,' he said.

'True,' I gasped, laughing, light-headed and euphoric in the mellow aftermath of orgasm.

I looked up at him and couldn't quite believe that he was still dressed, immaculate in his dress shirt. He climbed up onto the bed, tracing the design on my ankle before settling down alongside me and slipping an arm under my neck. He pulled me to him and kissed me hard, his lips tasting of my excitement. I closed my eyes.

'Are you okay?' he said.

I smiled sleepily. 'Oh yes,' I purred. 'Very.'

Adam laughed and stroked along my jawline with his finger. 'I love your tattoo.'

'A moment of madness.'

'Do you mean tonight or the tattoo?' he said.

'Both. That was amazing.'

He smiled. 'I'm glad you enjoyed it. Now, would you like to go back to the party,' he asked, 'or shall we stay here?'

Reaching up, I began to unbutton his shirt. 'I think we should stay here, don't you?' I said. 'It's got to be your turn now, Sir.'

Adam nodded. 'I'm not going to argue with that. Shall we get rid of the masks?'

I grinned. 'No, I really like them.'

He smiled and kissed me gently on the lips. 'Remind me. Who is the Dom again?'

I'd arrived at Maddie's birthday party a few hours earlier. It's one thing to go out in BDSM gear when you're part of a couple, but very, very different when you're on your own, driving through the leafy English countryside in broad daylight. I'd played it safe when I left the house and worn a camisole and jacket over my corset and net-skirt number, along with flat boots that would certainly help with the driving. The rest of my outfit for the evening was carefully tucked away in an overnight bag on the passenger seat.

The few times I'd met Maddie before – along with her husband – they had always struck me as really nice people and very supportive, encouraging and patient with me as a newbie. Back then, though, I had been with Max; things were very different now. I was on my own and looking for someone new, which was hard enough to do when I was looking for a vanilla relationship, but way, way harder when looking for someone I trusted enough to tie me up and spank me, or take a crop to me.

What happens is consensual and stylised, but it is still potentially dangerous, and though it is meant to hurt there is a huge difference between having someone who can Dominate and inflict a level of discomfort that you've both agreed on, and someone who wants to mindlessly hurt you either emotionally or physically. For me, and for most of the people involved in BDSM that I've met, it isn't about violence but about mutual pleasure.

So, what I was looking for in a Dom was a man who understood that BDSM is a complex and exciting, intense and mutually pleasurable game, where pleasure and pain are mixed, along with submission and domination and lifestyle choices. A good Dom is someone who can make you feel safe, take on the role of Master, and give you both pleasure. What I wasn't looking for was a wife beater or an out-and-out sadist. All this, and I was also looking for someone whom I wanted to spend time with. Someone I could have a real ongoing relationship with.

Although it may be hard from the outside to get your head around, BDSM is not about violence; it's about power and passion and, yes, some pain if that is what you're into, but not always. Finding the right Dom can take some time if you're after more than a casual encounter – and I was.

So there I was, all dressed up and en route to Maddie's place. As I got closer and closer to my destination, what had seemed like a good idea when Maddie and I had spoken on the phone, and even when I was getting ready, seemed increasingly crazy. What on earth was I thinking? I knew that over the course of the evening there would be lots of play going on, lots of bondage and other fun. How left out was I going to feel just watching, and if I didn't just watch who would I play with? Who would I trust? And just how much nerve was it going to take to walk into the party all on my own?

By the time I was a few miles from Maddie's place I had decided on a strategy. After all, I'd come this far. I'd just drop in for a little while so as not to offend Maddie, and then I'd make my excuses and leave. After all, in the future, when and if I found a new Dom, she might invite me again, and Maddie's parties were always fun. She was a good person to know. I tried to remember, when I'd been to her parties with Max, if there had been any single people around. The truth was I couldn't remember – which just goes to show how blinkered you get when you're in a relationship.

Before I left home, back when I had been planning on staying for the whole evening, I'd decided to arrive fairly early, hoping to get there before the party really got underway so that I could remind Maddie of her promise to look after me – not that I can't take care of myself, but I wasn't sure exactly how things worked as a single subbie.

I needn't have worried. I had barely parked and locked up my car before Maddie was out of the house and coming to meet me.

'I'm so glad you came,' she said, swooping down the drive to give me a big hug. She was wearing a camel coat over what looked like a pair of stiletto-heeled thigh boots. 'It's so nice to see you. I've got a couple of single Doms coming along tonight, possibly three – all vouched for, all lovely and ready to go. I'll give you the lowdown if you like the look of any of them. Oh, and there's a switch coming as well; she's bi, a real poppet, so you'll be just fine.'

A switch is someone who can be submissive or dominant depending on the circumstances or maybe how the mood takes them.

I looked at Maddie. She must have sensed my nervousness because she laughed and said, 'Don't worry. There will be loads of people to talk to and lots going on if you don't want to play. You know people will understand.'

Which was true, but it still felt odd walking in without Max. Maddie took me inside and showed me into a cloakroom just inside the front door where I could get changed and put my mask on. Everyone beyond the screen in the hall had to be masked, she said. House rules.

I'd never been to a masked party before, but I was thinking that being anonymous would really help with any nerves. I can be a bit of a wuss at times, whereas the woman in the cat mask and the killer red lipstick was a different matter altogether. She could be anyone she wanted, and just as confident as she wanted. Well, that was the plan on the drive over – now I was here, I wondered if I would be able to carry off the illusion.

I was just putting the finishing touches to my outfit and make-up when another woman, who I guessed was around my age, came in. She was tall and curvy, with long blonde hair swept up into a top knot, and wearing a glittery mask along with sheer harem pants and a tiny sequined top that barely contained a spectacular pair of breasts.

'Hi,' she said, extending her hand. 'I'm Kelly. Maddie told me to come and find you in case you panicked and made a run for it.' She laughed at my expression. 'She didn't really, but I'm on my own too – or at least, I am tonight. My partner can't make it, and I'd already promised to help Maddie with the food.' She grinned at me. 'Love the skirt.'

'Thank you. I'm Sarah,' I said. 'Maybe I can help you with the food?'

Kelly nodded. 'You can if you want to, but there's no pressure. Maddie said that you used to go out with Max?'

'Yes, that's right. We split up a little while ago.'

'Sorry to hear that,' Kelly said. 'I met him a couple of times here with Maddie. He was a really nice guy. Anyway, are you ready?'

I nodded. Although I knew Kelly was being nice and trying to put me at ease, talking about Max left me feeling even more raw and alone.

I had never been to a masked party before, let alone a masked BDSM party, so I had nothing to compare it to. Beyond the screens, in the living room, the early birds were already enjoying the cocktails and nibbles. Maddie's husband was the barman, while another man in a latex body suit and bow tie was acting as a waiter and handing round canapés. What struck me first was that everyone there had made an effort; they were all dressed up to the nines. Or undressed to the nines.

Maddie came over carrying two glasses of champagne. Divested of her overcoat she was wearing her party outfit – a tight-fitting patent-leather body suit with a peplum at hip level – a nod towards a frock coat, I guessed. She wore it with a silver-trimmed highwayman's mask and tricorn hat, all set off with her high-heeled thigh-high boots and a riding crop.

'Here we are, ladies,' she said, handing us a glass each. 'And I won't take no for an answer. I just wanted to let you know we've been planning games – proper party games: Musical Statues, Pass the Parcel; you know the kind of thing. I thought it would be fun. I just wanted to warn you. I'll be looking for volunteers.' She grinned.

'Actually, I was just offering to help Kelly with the food,' I said.

Maddie pulled a face. 'That's no excuse, and although it's very kind of you, I don't want either of you spending your whole evening in the kitchen.'

Kelly held her hands up. 'We won't be, but I just need to go and check on the state of play before anybody else arrives.'

Maddie waved her away. 'In that case, let me introduce you to some people, Sarah.'

She took my arm and guided me through the house.

At the far end of the sitting room were French windows that opened up onto a large gazebo where other guests were mingling. There were people in full evening dress with all kinds of erotic twists, and others who had obviously gone their own way. There was one woman in a fabulous satin purple corset, with a bustle, white fishnets and a tiara, accompanied by a man kitted out in something any self-respecting Musketeer would be happy to wear.

'I hadn't realised it was fancy dress,' I whispered to Maddie.

She laughed. 'It isn't. I just asked people to dress up. I wanted to make it special. I was thinking that a lot of people would go black tie, but actually this is so much more fun.'

'And special?'

'It's most certainly that,' said Maddie with a smile as we stepped out into the marquee. 'The dancing will be in here later,' she added as she led me towards a woman in a silver flapper dress with the most fabulous matching mask, topped with a pink plume.

In one hand the woman had a cigarette in a long ebony holder, in her other a long fine silver chain, on the far end of which was a fit-looking bald guy, probably in his mid-forties, who was naked except for a collar, a bow tie and a pair of very snug black shorts. His whole body was beautifully muscled and lightly tanned and, on slightly closer inspection, oiled. The chain the woman was holding was snapped onto a nipple ring, while the man sat at his mistress's feet. It was hard not to stare.

'Come on, let me introduce you,' said Maddie, following my gaze.

The party turned out to be really enjoyable. While more adult fun and games were planned for later on, in the early evening between food and dancing there were lots of traditional party games, which were a great way to start conversations with total strangers. Maddie's version of Pass the Parcel involved all sorts of interesting little somethings slipped between each layer of wrapping paper, ranging from flavoured condoms and naughty-shaped chocolates and little sachets of massage oil, through to the final prize of a pair of handcuffs. There was Stick the Tail on the Subbie and Musical Chairs, where many of the chairs were actually either a Dom's lap or a subbie on all fours.

I was in the middle of a game of Musical Chairs with just a few people left in when I was caught out between seats and cheered good naturedly off the floor. Hot and breathless and heady with laughter, I wandered outside into a little chill-out area in a courtyard garden just by the dining room to grab some fresh air and a cold drink.

True to their word, Kelly and Maddie had made sure I hadn't been alone for more than a few minutes since I'd arrived and I was having a really good time. But I was pretty certain that the tempo was soon set to change. Maddie had been to check on bedrooms that she had converted into playrooms for the party, and although I'd had a great evening and enjoyed the company, I hadn't met anyone I fancied playing with.

As I was having a drink and catching my breath I glanced up and caught sight of my reflection in one of the windows. Most of the red lipstick I'd put on when I'd arrived had worn off, and the mask and the light in the courtyard gave me a slightly otherworldly appearance. By some trick of the light and a flaw in the glass, when I moved in to take a closer look my reflection first of all doubled, then folded into itself and then vanished. I smiled. Maybe I should take it as an omen and head home before my singledom became all the more obvious.

It wasn't late. If I left now I could be back at home, bathed and curled up in bed in my PJs with a good book by midnight. I'd just say a quick goodbye to Maddie and Kelly and then slip away. As I was about to head back into the house I practically fell over a tall, blond-haired, masked man intent on coming out into the courtyard.

After a flurry of apologies he grinned at me. 'Making a getaway, are you?'

I laughed. 'I was thinking about it. I was just going to say my goodbyes. How about you?'

'I'm just out for a breath of fresh air.'

'Are you enjoying the party?'

He smiled. 'Hard to tell yet. I've not been here very long. I'm Adam, by the way.' He held out a hand.

'Sarah,' I said. 'Pleased to meet you.'

His handshake was firm and warm, and then he looked at me some more. 'I think I've just seen you, haven't I? Weren't you the woman running hell for leather round half a dozen chairs and ending up missing the lap of some man in rubber shorts?'

I reddened. 'That would be me.'

He grinned. 'You were robbed.'

And so we got talking, and to be honest I'm not sure what it was we talked about, but it seemed really easy and funny and we were both laughing a lot and then, after a few more minutes, Adam glanced back over his shoulder into the house and the rest of the guests, and it occurred to me that he was probably there with someone else, and that I was keeping him away from whoever it was. I felt a little foolish and even more alone.

'I suppose we should be getting back in,' Adam said, indicating towards the door.

I nodded, feeling a bit self-conscious. 'Yes, I suppose you're right. Nice to have met you.'

And then there was an odd, supercharged silence before we both started speaking at once.

Adam said, 'It's been great to chat with you, but I don't want to keep you away from your Dom.'

And I said, 'It's been brilliant talking to you, but I don't want to keep you away from your subbie.'

Although that probably wasn't exactly what we said, that was what we meant, and then we did that *Oh no, please, you go first* thing that you do when that happens. In the end, I said, 'Actually, I'm here on my own tonight. I split up with my Dom, Max, a little while back. It feels a bit weird being at something like this on my own.'

At which point Adam tipped his head to one side. His smile widened and he said, 'So you're *that* Sarah.'

I stared at him. '*That* Sarah? What does that mean? What have you heard?'

He smiled. 'Relax. Nothing bad, nothing bad at all. I think Maddie was planning to introduce us later. Seems like we've saved her the trouble.'

And then we carried on talking in the random way you do when you have an inkling that you fancy each other and you leap from tangent to tangent trying to find out as much as you can. So in not very long at all I discovered that Adam liked books and dogs and had travelled a lot, and that we lived an hour and a half away from each other and both liked Italian food, red wine and Ry Cooder, and had both been in Greece at the same time in 2005. Small world.

So that was how, an hour or so later, I found myself in one of Maddie's beautifully equipped playrooms, helping Adam out of his dress shirt and running my hands over his broad hairy chest, my mouth watering at the scent of his body and the strength in his muscular arms and shoulders as he pulled me to him.

His kisses made me shiver. I wanted him so much, my body filled with a strong dark animal desire. I could smell my arousal on his lips and see the need in his eyes. I wanted to give him as much pleasure and satisfaction as he had given me.

Adam began to unzip his trousers and my hands were there too, helping him to push them down, shuck them off and slide them to the bedroom floor. Underneath he was wearing close-fitting white jockey shorts that barely contained his excitement. The sight of his cock pressed hard and full against the fabric made my whole body tingle. He groaned with delight as I peeled them off and freed him.

Clothed, Adam was debonair and good company. Naked, Adam was gorgeous, with broad shoulders, narrow hips, a flat well-toned stomach that suggested more than a passing acquaintance with the gym, and long muscular legs. Very, very nice, bearing in mind I had expected to spend my evening alone.

Gently, I made my way down the bed and slipped onto the floor at his feet

He was hard, and as my hand closed around his shaft he let out a long, low, throaty moan. Up on my knees now I took him into my mouth, working his shaft with my lips, running my tongue up and down it and then trailing it oh-so-gently over the end, lapping at the eye and the little bridge of flesh just under the head.

He gasped and grabbed hold of my hair, guiding me up and down, up and down over his throbbing cock, my tongue and lips working in unison, one hand wrapped around the bottom of his shaft while I stroked his balls with the other.

'My God that feels so good,' he moaned. Adam sat back, easing himself down onto the bed with me still between his knees, hands working in tandem with my mouth. I could feel his excitement building towards the point of no return and so I slowed the pace, teasing out the moment, prolonging his pleasure, my lips just brushing the silken skin that covered his thick, swollen shaft, taking him to the brink and back, repaying him stroke for stroke for what he had given me.

Adam groaned. His breath was ragged and uneven and I could sense that he was getting closer and closer to the edge. Just as I thought he would let go, he pulled away from me. I gasped, feeling I had been robbed of the final prize.

'I want to fuck you so much, Sarah,' he murmured, pushing himself up onto his elbows.

Adam wasn't alone.

I smiled. 'Me too,' I whispered, as I crawled up onto the bed, feeling his rampant, hungry cock brushing my breasts and belly as I scrambled up till I had straddled him. There were condoms in a little bowl on the bedside cabinet. Adam leant over and took one. I undid it and between us we unrolled it over his shaft.

It was seconds then before he was inside me. I felt my body opening to him, eager to take him, eager to share the moment. The feeling of his cock sliding home, deep inside me, made me sigh with pure delight.

I began to move against him, setting a rhythm, relishing the way he filled me. I had assumed that it wouldn't be long before Adam came, but I was oh-so-wrong; before I could topple him over the edge, he grabbed my hips to still me and then began to move again, more slowly this time, lifting his pelvis so that he brushed up against me, his fingers joining in, teasing my clitoris, the lightest touch, the softest caress.

I looked down at him, seeing his lazy, horny grin, against all the odds feeling my own excitement begin to rekindle. And now, without a word, it became a competition.

I started to move, tightening my sex rhythmically around his shaft, drawing him deep, holding him firm. Adam groaned and plunged deeper still, his fingers working the soft engorged bud of my clitoris. Oh, he was good – he knew exactly how to touch me and when. We were both riding the wave now, finding our rhythm, him holding back, me gaining on him fast.

With each stroke, each touch, I could feel the pleasure building deep in my belly, like a summer storm, feel him so very, very close to the edge. And then I was there on the edge of the precipice with him, tumbling, falling, the deep rhythmic spasms of my orgasm triggering his. Adam cried out as he finally came, hard and fast, pushing into me again and again, his thrusts ragged now, pushing deeper and deeper. Then finally we collapsed onto the bed, both breathless, both glowing white-hot. I rolled off him and we lay side by side. Him with his arm around my neck, still masked, breathing hard, totally and utterly spent.

We dozed for a while, spooning and snuggling together, which felt fabulous. Adam slipped his arm around me and pulled me close, his face pressed into my neck, kissing me gently as we both fell asleep.

It would have been nice if at that point we'd taken the masks off and spent the rest of the night together, or maybe – still masked – gone back out to re-join the others at the party, but that wasn't what happened. When we woke a little while later Adam got up, took a robe off the back of the door and went to get us both a drink. When he came back he started to get dressed. I was a bit surprised, and said so. I suppose I had been hoping that we could spend some more time together.

'Me too. I'm really sorry about this,' Adam said, 'but I've got to go. I've got a breakfast meeting in

Birmingham tomorrow morning and then I'm flying on to Germany.' He paused as he fastened his cufflinks. 'I really hadn't expected to meet anyone tonight.'

I was still on the bed, watching him finish getting dressed. I smiled. 'Me neither.'

'I'm really sorry that I can't stay. Can I see you again?' he asked.

I nodded. 'I'd like that.'

Adam glanced into the mirror, slipping on his jacket and raking his fingers through his hair to try and tidy it. 'Good. Can we sort a date out when I get back?'

'Fine.'

'Great. So is it time to take the masks off?' he asked, turning back to face me.

I laughed. 'No, keep them on. I'll look forward to seeing you for real next time.'

'I thought tonight was pretty real.' He grinned, eyes bright with mischief. 'But yes, okay, you're on. Can I have your number –?' He hesitated, tapping his pockets. 'Oh, hang on. I haven't got my phone with me. I left it in the car.'

'I left mine in my bag in the changing room.'

'Okay, just don't go anywhere,' Adam said, as he headed back out into the corridor. 'I'll go and get it.'

He didn't take long to get back. 'So,' he said, pulling his phone out of his pocket. 'Shoot.'

I gave him my number.

'Would you like mine?' he asked as he tucked the phone back into his pocket.

I smiled. 'I'd love it, but despite appearances I'm a bit old-fashioned. I think I'd prefer it if you rang me. I'm not keen on being the one doing the chasing.'

Adam nodded. 'Fair enough. I'll call you in the week once I'm back from Germany.' And then he paused, his tone softening. 'I've had a really good evening, Sarah. I don't want to go, but I have to. I arrived with no expectations – meeting you has been very special. Thank you.' And then he leaned in close and kissed me gently.

'Call me,' I said as he opened the bedroom door.

'I will,' he said. 'See you soon.' He tapped his pocket and then he was gone.

I left not long after and got home in the wee small hours as the dark was lightening into the new day. I was asleep as soon as my head hit the pillow and I dreamed of men in masks and Pass the Parcel.

Chapter Two

'We're so glad that you could make it. Would you like to come through, Sarah? May I call you Sarah?' said my hostess, Gill, who was guiding me by the elbow. 'I hope your room is all right. I'm rather envious. It's such a lovely hotel. We often have afternoon tea here. And the spa is lovely –' Gill was a small, busy, lovely woman, probably in her early sixties and dressed head to toe in fuchsia pink. She glanced at her watch as we headed through a set of doors marked *Private*. 'I'm not sure where everyone else has got to. I thought it was supposed to be seven for seven-thirty. The other judges should be here by now,' she said. She looked at her watch again, as if that might summon them up. 'They're probably in the bar,' she said with a wry smile. 'Anyway, we're so pleased you're here.'

'Thank you for inviting me,' I began.

Gill waved the words away. 'Don't thank me,' she said. 'We're just delighted that you said you'd stand in for Sue, especially at the last minute.' She laughed.

'Trust me, guest judges aren't that easy to come by at the eleventh hour. We're just so pleased that you said yes.'

Why wouldn't I? The organisers had offered to pay for a first-class rail fare and a night in a lovely hotel if I would cover for one of their judges for a short-story competition and come to the prize-giving dinner to announce the winners and present the first prize. The event had been sponsored by a local business, so the judging panel consisted of a guest writer, someone from the local charity that the competition was fundraising for, and someone on the board of the company involved. Apparently it was an annual event, and the tickets for the dinner, the raffle and the publicity it attracted all helped to boost the charity's funds.

The writer I was standing in for – who was a good friend and had recommended me – had had to pull out because of a family crisis and had already done most of the heavy lifting. By the time I got to see the competition entries they had been narrowed down to a very short shortlist, so it was just a question of expressing an opinion and giving marks on the final few, which would then be totted up to decide on the overall winner. Given the short notice, I hadn't had to go to any of the meetings, and my decisions and thoughts on the final selection had been sent in by email. So it was hardly an onerous task, and having just delivered my new book to my publisher, I really rather fancied a night out. It was the perfect excuse to dress up.

The organiser had said I could bring a plus one if I wanted, but I'd declined – there were people I could invite but I quite liked the idea of having a little time to myself with room service, and the promise of the hotel spa the next morning was tempting.

With Gill in the lead we headed into a small ante-room. There was champagne and orange juice, as well as a tray of canapés on a side table, along with some cards and flyers explaining the charity's work, with others from the company sponsoring the event. I picked one up to take a look.

Gill smiled. 'Feel free to take some with you and spread the word. We've been working so hard to get this event off the ground. The company that sponsors us has been fabulous, but every penny helps. Have you met the other judges? Jonathon Smith? Peter Hawkes?'

I shook my head.

'Oh, you'll love them. They're both such nice men. When we started all this they really hit it off, which makes working with them a real joy. They're great fun, the two of them, and put in so much effort to make sure that our events work. And then there's Anna – she's our events coordinator and is going to be master of ceremonies for this evening.' Gill took another look at her watch. 'Actually, I'm surprised she isn't here already. She is usually first to arrive for everything. Anyway, the plan is we've got a few announcements to make before we get to the competition winners – people who've raised money, two sponsored walkers, and a man who ran in the last marathon who is going to present us with a cheque.'

She reached into her handbag. 'Oh, before I forget, I've got a programme here for you. And then we'll announce the winners of the competition and present the prizes, and then I think Jonathon is going to say a few words about our organisation and his company's links with it, then Peter will give a vote of thanks, and then we'll finally have dinner.'

She laughed. 'By which time we will all well and truly have earned it. Fairly straightforward stuff, really –' Gill paused and looked down at her notes. 'Oh, and one more thing. I know Anna was going to ask you but as she's not here – and I appreciate we're springing it on you, so please feel free to say no – we were wondering if you might like to say a few words about the competition entries?'

Do I need to tell you that Adam hadn't phoned me since the party? The first couple of days after Maddie's get-together I assumed he didn't ring because he was stuck in meetings and probably still in Germany – although I did hope that just maybe he might find the time to call anyway. By the end of the week I was thinking that maybe – possibly –

either he hadn't got back yet or he was weighing up whether he or I were really interested in meeting up again and taking what we had started any further. Halfway through the second week I'd taken the hint and more or less given up any hope that Adam would contact me again, although every time the phone rang and I didn't recognise the number I still thought there was a chance it might be him. It seemed a shame he didn't ring again as we'd got on so well. But who knew what he had thought on reflection? Whatever the reason, there was nothing I could do about it.

Was I hurt or upset? Maybe, just a little bit, for the first week, because we had both had such a good time together and really seemed to hit it off, but not enough to dwell too long on it. We were consenting adults and we'd had a great evening. Some things you just have to chalk up to experience. We'd had fun.

So I was back on the lookout for Mr Right. It had to have been at least a couple of months since Maddie's party and since then I'd met up with a few possible Doms, but no one who rang any bells or I had the slightest interest in playing with or seeing again. I wasn't looking for Mr Right tonight, though. Tonight was all about work, with the prospect of time off in the spa the next day, so I declined the champagne I was offered and took a glass of orange juice from the tray instead.

It was the first night since Maddie's party that I'd been anywhere that required formal dress, and I'd pulled out all the stops and *really* dressed up, although obviously my outfit was a little more restrained than at Maddie's do. I'd chosen a long black evening dress that fitted me like a glove and was sprinkled here and there with tiny jet beads that glittered slightly when they caught the light, and I accessorised with a gold-and-black wrap, along with strappy high heels and a little clutch bag. I'd also twisted my hair up into a knot and teased out a few tendrils to frame my face.

It was an outfit that I'd usually dress up with my diamanté earrings, but it had occurred to me when I'd been packing, and again a few minutes earlier upstairs in my hotel room as I was getting ready, that the last time I'd seen them was when Adam had taken them off and carefully slipped them into the pocket of his dinner jacket for safe keeping.

Which had given me pause for thought. Maybe I should give Maddie a ring and ask if she would contact him for me? I might not be seeing Adam again, but I'd quite like to see my earrings.

'So,' Gill was saying. 'Would you be happy to say a few words about the competition entries?'

I was just agreeing when the rest of the judges and their partners, and Anna, the MC for the evening, along with a half a dozen other people, arrived en masse. They were a noisy, talkative bunch who obviously all knew each other well.

Gill took it upon herself to introduce me to them all. It was one of those moments when you just know that, despite everyone's good intentions, there isn't a snowball's chance in hell of remembering more than one or possibly two or three names at the very most. Nevertheless, Gill ploughed on and steered me into the middle of this cheerful mêlée.

'Sarah, this is Peter, he's the current chairman of our charity, and this is his wife, Linda. And this is Anna, who is MC-ing, and this John, her husband, and this is –' The names seemed to go on and on in a bit of a blur of smiling and handshaking, until we reached one of the men who had been finishing an aside to one of the other guests as Gill introduced us. He turned as she spoke and held out a hand.

'And this is Jonathon,' Gill said. 'He owns the company that is sponsoring this evening's event.'

Our eyes met and for an instant there was a flash of recognition that momentarily threw me. Neither of us spoke. His name didn't ring any bells. It struck me that I might be mistaken. Maybe he just reminded me of someone else … He smiled; obviously he'd had much the same thought.

'And this is Janie,' continued Gill, smiling at the two of them. Janie was tall and slim, a striking blonde, dressed in a fabulous blue sheath dress that accentuated a model figure, great tan and a gym-honed body. She couldn't be more than thirty and had a really warm, engaging smile.

'Lovely to meet you,' she said, catching hold of my hand to shake it, followed a millisecond later by Jonathon saying and doing much the same thing. As I touched him and our eyes met again I was even more convinced that we'd met before, but I couldn't place his face. Nevertheless, there was an instant and uncanny feeling that I knew him.

We exchanged pleasantries and a bit of small talk and I tried not to stare at Jonathon, annoyed that I couldn't remember where I knew him from, meanwhile Gill was talking to Janie, who had her arm through Jonathon's. Obviously, she kept him on a tight rein, I thought. As the conversation moved on I noticed that she was wearing a wedding ring, but Jonathon wasn't.

'I've read your latest book,' Janie was saying. 'I really enjoyed it.'

I smiled and thanked her, and told her I had just delivered a new one. 'Oh, then I'll be looking out for it. Jonathon let me read the shortlisted stories,' she continued, brightly. 'I thought they were really good. We were so pleased that so many people entered.'

'There were some great stories,' I began.

'Yes,' Janie said, 'but –' She took a quick look in Jonathon's direction. He laughed, taking a glass of champagne from the tray and handing it to her.

'But,' he said, 'Janie thinks we should have picked a different winner. And wanted me to change my mind.' His tone was teasing and familiar.

Janie pulled a face. 'But you didn't, though, did you?'

He held up his hands. 'I already told you, the judges' decision is final. Despite any attempts at bribery.'

She turned to me. 'Take no notice of him. Actually, I thought all of the top three were good. I just liked the runner-up better, that's all.'

'And don't I just know it,' said Jonathon, feigning exasperation.

They had an ease about them that I envied. Glancing round the anteroom I began to regret not bringing a plus one. It hadn't occurred to me that the top table might be all couples, but I was sure I'd be fine. It wouldn't be the first time I'd been somewhere on my own, but some things just highlighted my singledom.

Meanwhile I caught Jonathon smiling at me and I smiled back. I knew that eventually I'd remember where I knew him from. Janie was busy talking about a book she was reading that she thought I might like, and was trying to tell me about it without giving too much of the plot away. I had really warmed to her and she was saying that perhaps she could get me over to speak to her book group when Gill on the far side of the gathering clapped her hands.

'Ladies and gentlemen, I really think we should be making a move and going upstairs.'

There was a murmur of agreement and people started to move. Gill fell in with me and we made our way out into the foyer along with the others. The vestibule was still fairly crowded with guests, all making their way up to the prize-giving dinner.

The stairs were busy.

My evening gown is lovely but it wouldn't be the first time I'd inadvertently walked up the front of a long dress while wearing high heels and stumbled, so I grabbed hold of the banister with one hand and lifted my skirt with the other. As I did, I looked over towards Gill, who was asking me about my latest book, and at the same time I caught a glimpse of the expression on Jonathon's face.

It was a study in surprise and recognition. He was looking at my bare legs – more specifically he was looking at my tattoo: the flurry of tiny stars that cascades down towards my ankle – and when he looked up and caught my gaze, I saw the realisation in his eyes. His big blue eyes. At which point my mind helpfully joined the dots and I knew exactly where we had met before and when. Only of course when we had met last time he had been called Adam. *Adam.* It took all my presence of mind not to say it out loud.

I had a vivid flashback. The last time I had seen Adam, and Adam had seen that tattoo, he had been kneeling at the end of the bed, pressing kisses to my inner thighs, my knees, my ankles, before kissing each little star in turn and then working his way back up.

Jonathon did a double take and then opened his mouth to say something, just as Janie slipped her arm through his. 'I'm absolutely famished,' she said, beaming up at him. 'How long do you think the speeches are going to take?'

'Not too long, I hope,' he said, still looking across at me. Between us we were in danger of causing a traffic jam.

Janie looked heavenwards. 'Oh, come on. Don't give me that. We both know they'll be ages,' she joked.

Janie was beautiful, funny, attractive and at least ten years younger than Jonathon – the perfect arm candy for someone so obviously successful. Don't get me wrong, this isn't sour grapes. I just wondered why on earth he was playing away when he had someone as lovely as Janie at home.

It occurred to me that maybe she wasn't into BDSM; it wouldn't be the first time I'd come across a husband or wife who had strayed to feed a hunger that couldn't be met by a vanilla partner, but it was the first time it had happened to me, and I was perturbed and uncomfortable, and to be honest Jonathon plummeted in my estimation. Other women's men are off-limits as far as I'm concerned, and had I known Jonathon was married he would have been a no-go area from the start. I looked away. It left a sour taste in my mouth.

Trouble was, even with Janie there, I could feel the little flutter of attraction between us, and tried my level best to ignore it. I made a point of dropping my expression into neutral and turning my attention back to Gill.

Climbing the stairs, I could still feel Jonathon's eyes following me, still trying to make eye contact, but I did my best to avoid him. I was annoyed at being duped as well as sad. It had been such a perfect evening at Maddie's. And then I thought about the time I'd spent wondering if he would call, wondering if he had thought about me or enjoyed the evening as much I had, when all the time he was married.

However, being cross wasn't going to help anyone tonight – I'd been invited to the dinner to do a job, not mope about being conned. It was a good lesson.

All I had to do was get through this evening's dinner. All I had to do was keep schtum, be polite but not too familiar, and get through it – after all, how hard could it be? I certainly wasn't going to bring the conversation round to adultery or a night of light bondage, so I was certain I could carry it off and chalk the whole thing down to experience.

The top table for the judges and their guests was on a small raised dais at the end of the hall. We were all arranged along the back and sides of the table so that we looked out over the room and the rest of the diners, and sod's law being what it is, they had put me on one of the ends so that every time I looked up, my natural line of sight took me straight to the happy couple – who seemed to be having a great time, but not so great that Jonathon didn't keep glancing in my direction.

The last thing I wanted to hear was any lame excuse about how his wife didn't understand him – not that Jonathon was likely to actually say anything like that there and then. I was feeling prickly, though, so while I was polite and didn't ignore him, I tried not to meet his eye too often, and basically not make too much of it.

Everyone else on the table was relaxed and chatty, which made things easier, but there was definitely a whisper of an undercurrent that maybe only I could feel. Jonathon was just a fraction too far away to easily engage me in conversation, but I could still feel him looking, trying out a smile and eye contact, while Janie was terribly jolly and animated, making sure everyone was involved in the conversation, including me. She was quick and witty and making everyone laugh. It was easy to like her. Even so, I found it hard to relax and decided I wouldn't be sorry when the evening was over.

Anna, the MC for the evening, checked everyone at the table was ready, then got to her feet and tapped a knife on a glass to call the hall to order. There were lots of tables in the room and around one hundred guests, all decked out in evening dress – a mix of supporters of the charity, prize-winners and people who had come to present cheques.

After she had welcomed everyone, Anna introduced herself and each of us, and then Peter, the chairman, talked about the valuable work the organisation did and how very much he appreciated the links with local businesses and the opportunities that such collaboration brought. At which point he introduced Jonathon. As Jonathon got to his feet our eyes met, and for an instant we made a connection. He smiled at me. A big, secret smile. A smile that promised more. And what was worse was that Janie saw him, and saw the look that passed between us.

I was totally wrong-footed and, unable to hide my surprise, felt my colour rising. I looked away. Meanwhile Janie turned to me and smiled, and *sotto voce* said, 'I didn't know that you and Jonathon knew each other.'

She'd got that from a look? I was thrown. 'I think I may have met him once before,' I blustered, as he adjusted his jacket and reached into his pocket to take out his notes. As he did I saw a moment of surprise on his face and then a smile. Cringing inwardly, I guessed what it was that had caused it. Assuming that he hadn't had his dinner jacket cleaned since the party at Maddie's, the likelihood was that Jonathon had just rediscovered my earrings.

He looked at me again. This time he grinned and, leaning down, whispered something to Janie. I didn't dare look at them; instead I closed my eyes, praying that he had the good sense to leave the earrings where they were and not pull them out along with the prompt cards.

Regaining his composure, Jonathon turned his attention to his audience and began to speak, thanking everyone for their help and kindness and saying how much he and his company enjoyed their involvement, then thanking Anna and thanking Janie for all the support she had given him. She beamed and patted Jonathon on the arm, a little self-conscious and shy. He smiled down at her and she looked up at him and nodded proudly.

I looked away and tried hard not to groan; God, this was awful. She was so nice. After that, I really have no idea what it was he said. All I could think about was the quizzical look on Janie's face and the way she had looked at me. I had no idea what it was she had seen in Jonathon's expression that I hadn't, but I knew that it gave away a lot more than I was comfortable with – or was that just my conscience talking?

Awards were given, cheques presented and then Anna invited me to say a few words about the short-story competition before announcing the winner. I'd been so perturbed by recognising Jonathon that I'd totally forgotten that they had asked me to speak.

Anna handed me the microphone. Getting to my feet I took a breath and looked out across a sea of expectant faces. I thanked the judges and then found myself talking about the need for honesty and trust and truth between an author and their readership. How you have to build up a bond and deliver what you've promised to the people who matter most – those who have invested time and thought and emotion in the thing you have created, and how the winning story had done just that by delivering on its promise. I couldn't meet Jonathon's gaze, because those things aren't just important between writers and their readers. Then I talked about what an honour it had been to be asked to stand in for my friend, and how hard it had been to choose the eventual winner.

At which point Anna stood up and handed me the envelope containing the winner's name. I paused and then announced the first prize. There was a lot of whooping and squealing from a table close by, people clapped, and a young woman got up, looking surprised and a bit shellshocked and then delighted as she headed up to the dais to collect her prize.

To make it easier I walked round to the front of the table, followed a second or two later by Jonathon. I congratulated the winner and gave her a hug, while Jonathon shook her hand and presented her with a trophy and the book tokens that she'd won.

I concentrated my efforts on gushing to the winner about how wonderful her story was.

'Can we talk?' Jonathon said as she turned to go back to her table.

'I don't think so,' I said in an undertone.

He looked confused. 'I thought we had a great time,' he began.

'We did, but I don't cheat on people,' I said, looking pointedly at Janie, who was still sitting down at the table, deep in conversation with Peter beside her.

Jonathon looked genuinely surprised and, following my gaze, said, 'It's not like that with me and Janie.'

Here we go, I thought. He's going to tell me now that she doesn't mind or that she doesn't understand him. But before either of us could say anything else, Anna was back on her feet, tapping her glass again, thanking everyone and announcing that dinner was about to be served. With that, a phalanx of waitresses streamed out of the service doors by the kitchen and started delivering the first course.

'Let's talk later,' he said.

'No thanks,' I said, heading back to my seat.

I felt better for having said something, even if I hadn't said much, and decided that once we'd eaten I'd make my excuses and head back upstairs. I didn't think now that the prize-giving was over that I would be missed.

Dinner was delicious. Jonathon tried to catch my eye once or twice, but I just smiled and carried on talking to the diners who were seated closer to me. Once we'd had coffee I quietly told Gill that I didn't feel very well and planned an early night. I'd done what was asked of me, and I didn't want any fuss, so I planned to make a discreet exit. Gill said she would make my apologies. So while everyone else was in full flow, I slipped away. As I got out onto the landing I was surprised and a bit taken aback to find that Janie had followed me.

'Sarah, wait,' she said. 'You're not going, are you?' She didn't wait for me to reply. 'I wanted to ask you how you know Jonathon.'

I shrugged, trying to quell a growing sense of panic while coming up with something that was pleasant but evasive. The last thing I wanted was a spat with his wife. 'I'm not sure now,' I lied. 'Some social thing. A party maybe.'

She nodded but wasn't going to be shaken off. 'Only he seems quite keen on you. He's been trying to attract your attention all evening.'

I felt my colour rising.

'Ah,' I said, playing for time, wondering what to say next. 'Didn't he remember where we'd met?'

She raised her eyebrows. 'No, he seems a bit vague as well. I need to say something to you before you go back in there. Sarah –'

I closed my eyes, waiting for whatever it as that was coming next. Did nice girls slap women who had slept with their husbands or was it something much, much worse?

'You should tell him that it doesn't matter where you met him before, just that you'd like to see him again.'

I swung round and stared at her. 'What?'

'Oh, come on, I'm not stupid. It's obvious you fancy each other. He's been so miserable the last year or so. To be honest, I've been really worried about him since his divorce.'

There are not many times in life when my mouth has really, truly dropped open, but this was one of them.

'I can't keep on being his plus one,' Janie said, pressing on, apparently oblivious to my surprise. 'My husband doesn't mind, but people are beginning to talk and it's not fair. Jonathon is lovely, but he needs someone of his own.'

'I thought you were married, you and Jonathon,' I blustered.

Janie laughed. 'Good God, no. I love him dearly but he'd drive me crazy – I mean, not that there is anything wrong with him. No, I used to work for him years ago. He introduced me to my husband; we've been friends ever since. He was in bits when his wife left him and it's taken him a while to get it back together. He's such a lovely man. It really hit him hard when she went. She met someone online that she used to go to school with. Apparently they'd always had a thing for each other. He was devastated.'

I nodded, totally wrong-footed and perturbed that I had read the situation so badly. She grinned.

'He said that you wouldn't talk to him because you didn't go out with men who cheat.'

I reddened. 'I thought you were a couple.'

She laughed. 'Very commendable, but he is totally free, totally single, and I reckon if the conversation I had with him earlier is anything to go by, he fancies the pants off you.'

I laughed; if only Janie knew …

'Are you okay?' asked Gill as Janie and I both made our way back to the table. 'I thought you were going upstairs?' she said quietly.

'I think I just needed a bit of fresh air,' I said as I caught Jonathon's eye. He was making his way around the table towards me. This time his smile was undisguised. 'I might go later,' I said.

'Oh, that's good,' Gill said. 'We're hoping to get some photographs for the local paper with our prize-winner. Jonathon, would you like to keep Sarah company while I go and find everyone?'

'I'd be delighted,' he said.

I smiled.

'We just need everyone back on the dais.' Gill laughed. 'We should have done this before we finished dinner. It's like herding cats. If you'll excuse me, I'll go and round everyone up. Please just stay there,' she joked, waving us into our seats.

'I think I may have something of yours,' Jonathon said as soon as she was gone, dipping a hand into his jacket pocket. I smiled as he produced my earrings. 'You are even more gorgeous without your mask,' he added.

'You too,' I said.

'Maybe we could find somewhere quiet to have a drink and catch up.'

'Gill told us to stay where we are, and aren't you here with Janie?' I asked.

He laughed. 'I am, but it was Janie who insisted I come over here and talk to you.'

'Remind me. Who is the Dom again?' I said.

Jonathon leaned in and kissed me very gently. 'I am,' he said. 'And I intend to prove it to you later.'

One brief brush of his lips set my pulse racing.

When the photos were all taken and the guests had all gone, Jonathon got Janie a cab and then came back to join me in the residents' lounge.

'I need to explain a couple of things – I'm really sorry I didn't ring you,' he said once he was settled. 'I had my phone stolen at the airport. I tried ringing Maddie when I got back from Germany but she wouldn't give me your number.'

I stared at him. 'Really?'

I tried to think back to how Maddie and I had left things after the party. I remembered I'd emailed to thank her for a great evening and she'd emailed me back, and that was the last I'd heard from her. 'I've got no idea why she would do that.'

'Me neither, but it doesn't matter now,' he said. 'We were obviously meant to meet up again.' As he spoke, Jonathon leaned over and ran his finger along the inside of my wrist. 'I'd really like to get to know you better, but at the moment what I'd really like to do is tie you up and carry on where we left off.' He paused. 'I know the rules are different away from Maddie's party, out in the real world, so if it's too much, too soon, then that's fine, but I'd like to see you again, whatever you decide.'

I smiled up at him. 'Funnily enough, I've got a room booked for tonight.'

He grinned. 'Me too. So what are you saying?'

'That if you hadn't asked me I would probably have asked you,' I said. The air between us was crackling with expectation.

'Very forward of you,' he said.

'You'd have had to work for it.'

He nodded. 'So, your place or mine?'

'How about we go and take a look and decide who has the nicest room?' I said.

He grinned. 'I'm game.'

* * *

Jonathon won hands down. He had a suite and a bottle of champagne cooling in an ice bucket on a long low table between two huge leather sofas. The room was luxurious, softly lit, with a huge bed, and it was obvious as soon as we stepped across the threshold that we weren't leaving in a hurry.

Chapter Three

As the door closed Jonathon kissed me long and slow, his lips soft and eager, his tongue brushing my lips, seeking a way in, reminding me just how good he was with it. I relished the sensation of his arms around me. I could feel my body responding to his touch.

'I'm so glad I found you again,' he said.

'I was thinking exactly the same thing,' I replied.

'You want to play?' Jonathon said, pulling away.

I grinned. 'Yes, Sir.'

'Impressive,' he said. 'Are you always this well behaved?'

I raised an eyebrow. 'What do you think?'

He laughed. 'Get undressed for me. I want to see you –'

He poured a glass of champagne and made his way over to the bed. Sitting back among the pillows, Jonathon raised his glass.

'And I don't like to be kept waiting,' he said, his expression and demeanour subtly changing from dinner guest and judge to Dom.

It took me a moment or two to catch up. There is a change of mindset and pace when you begin to play, a choice to be made that is about accepting submission, letting the scene unfold and putting yourself in someone else's hands. You can always snap out of role and stop, but if you want to play you have to cross the line, and there is a moment when you take that step into that other, darker, more compelling, altogether edgier place.

I looked down at Jonathon and took in the details that had been denied me when he was masked. He was handsome in a sharp, rather craggy way. What the mask had hidden was a broad open face with good cheekbones, a long nose and a web of laughter lines around those big blue eyes. His gaze was fixed now, a smile playing on his lips while he waited to see if I would comply. I had the choice.

Very slowly I lifted my arms, undid the clasp at the back of my dress and shimmied it down over one shoulder. I took my time, knowing that I had his undivided attention. Under my dress I was wearing a black lacy bra and matching panties, sheer and soft. I slipped the dress off the other shoulder and slowly let it slide down to my waist, pressing it lower, running my hands down over my own body.

Jonathon made a soft throaty sound of approval and appreciation. I smiled.

The dress slid to the floor. Beneath it my black lace underwear was a stark contrast to my pale skin.

I slid my fingers under the straps of my bra, channelling a lifetime's memories of burlesque dancers and pin-up poses, relishing the sense of power it gave me as I could see him hooked on every move, every turn. I began to writhe just a little as I slid off first one strap and then the other.

He smiled and licked his lips. I ran one hand down over the curve of my breast, cradling them both while my other hand reached round to unfasten the catch. It took a second or two before it opened and I could tease the wisp of black silk out from under my arm and let it fall to join the dress. I began to dance slowly, to an unheard tune, letting my hands work over my body, cupping my breasts, before running them down over my stomach to the neatly trimmed triangle that was visible through the sheer fabric of my panties. As I slid my hand between my legs Jonathon gasped.

'Come here,' he said, beckoning me close, his voice thick with desire and excitement. I crept up onto the end of the bed, catlike, on all fours. 'Stay there,' he said. 'Just like that.'

And then he was alongside me, stroking me, caressing the generous curves of my backside, sliding between my legs, brushing my sex still covered by the fine silky fabric.

'I'm torn between wanting to spank you and wanting to fuck you,' he murmured.

I didn't need to remind him that he could do both. He spread my legs a little wider and very gently began to tap at my sex with an open palm, as if he was spanking it. He tapped hard and then softer, then harder again. I felt the vibration echo through me, each little tap adding to the sensation. It was an odd feeling and yet at the same time compelling. I found myself tilting my pelvis to chase his touch, the tap-tap of his flat open palm … Against expectation, I could feel my excitement start to build. He eased my panties down and began to tap harder, his other hand on the small of my back, holding me in place. His fingers slipped inside me and then out, then lower to find my clitoris. I moaned softly, pushing myself back onto his caress, more eager with every passing second.

'Do you want me to fuck you?' he asked.

'Yes,' I said.

He laughed. 'Ask nicely.'

'Yes, please, Sir,' I said.

I heard the familiar sound of a condom packet being opened, and then the gentle brush of the head of his cock against my inner thighs as it made its way higher, seeking my sex, as hungry and eager as I was. For an instant my body resisted him, closed tight against his cock, and then it opened as he slid deep into me, taking my breath away as he pressed his cock home.

He began to move and I matched his rhythm, then he leaned over me so I could feel his belly and chest against my back while his fingers reached between my legs to seek out the hard swollen bud of my clitoris, and I, wanting to give him measure for measure, put my hand back between my legs so that I could cup his balls and stroke his shaft where it met and slid into my body. He gasped as my fingers brushed his scrotum, and let out a long sigh of pleasure.

His touch was just as compelling. I pursued it, moving to milk every last touch, losing my concentration on the mission to caress him as my own excitement built like a fluttering, hungry pulse deep inside me. His fingers worked tirelessly. I groaned. He knew exactly what was needed and I knew that I was losing it. I was heading closer and closer to the edge and then, all at once, I was there, tumbling, falling, my sex closing rhythmically around his cock like a hungry, eager mouth, my whole body alight with pleasure. Then, seconds later, I felt his strokes getting stronger and stronger, closer and closer together, as he followed me into the abyss, his breath coming in great bursts. Finally I felt the pulse of his orgasm deep, deep in my sex. Jonathon gasped, groaning, hot and raw as he came, his strokes matching mine.

The strokes became more ragged as we both milked the last sensations, riding the final waves until all that existed was the sound of our breathing. Spent and sweating, we both collapsed down onto the bed.

Rolling over, I glanced across at him. 'So, would you like my telephone number?'

He grinned. 'I think so – maybe you could write it on a piece of paper this time.'